CREATIVE**TAPPING**
FOR**MODERN**GUITAR

Discover Creative Guitar Tapping Techniques & Licks For Any Musical Genre

KRISTOF**NEYENS**

FUNDAMENTAL**CHANGES**

Creative Tapping For Modern Guitar

Discover Creative Guitar Tapping Techniques & Licks For Any Musical Genre

ISBN: 978-1-78933-201-8

Published by **www.fundamental-changes.com**

www.fundamental-changes.com

Twitter: @guitar_joseph

Over 11,000 fans on Facebook: **FundamentalChangesInGuitar**

Instagram: **FundamentalChanges**

For over 350 Free Guitar Lessons with Videos Check Out

www.fundamental-changes.com

Cover Image Copyright: Peter Fizgal. Used by permission

Contents

Introduction

Tapping or two-handed tapping has long been widely used in genres such as Metal and Math Rock, but has many applications in other genres. In this book, we'll be looking at lots of musical and creative ways to use both hands on the fretboard, and you'll discover new techniques you can use, regardless of the genre of music you play.

Tapping sometimes has a stigma attached to it – perhaps viewed as being too flashy – or is simply overlooked as a technique. But, in recent times, tapping has made a resurgence with the growth of the more technically driven guitar movement, so it is a technique worth adding to your arsenal of ideas. I advise you to think of it purely as a way of playing notes in a lick or phrase that would otherwise be out of reach. Like any technique for guitar, tapping is just another tool to bring your musical ideas to light and can enhance any style of music.

If you're completely new to tapping and it seems like an advanced technique, don't worry – I break down everything as the book progresses. We'll begin with the absolute basics, and the content here is accessible for players of all levels. In fact, you'll be able to use tapping in your playing instantly because each chapter begins with simple ideas before building into more complex licks.

If you're an advanced musician, don't worry either – there are dozens of new ideas for you to get your teeth into and plenty of challenges to stretch your playing.

Throughout this book it will become clear that overdrive or distortion are not necessary to make tapping sound great. Most of the examples here were recorded with a clean tone using my trusty H.S. Anderson guitars. These instruments have vintage-voiced, low output pickups and couldn't be further away from the types of guitars used by the Metal gods. In fact, I urge you to practice this technique with a clean sound, even if you'll add distortion later, to make sure you play everything as cleanly as possible.

In Chapter One I'll show you how to get started with tapping. We'll cover the fundamentals, including which finger to use to tap, how to dampen the strings, how to create finger independence, and how to develop control with both hands on the fretboard.

In Chapter Two you will learn tapping licks you can instantly add to your vocabulary. By combining tapping with other techniques, like sliding and bending, you'll learn how to implement these licks in a wide range of musical styles.

Chapter Three is all about chords and fretboard visualization. We will begin with a linear approach to triads in one octave and build up to 7th chords and less common arpeggios stretching over multiple octaves. These ideas will dramatically improve your finger independence and fluency.

In Chapter Four more fingers of the picking hand are introduced and, like Chapter Two, we'll begin with some licks you can instantly add to your vocabulary.

Chapter Five provides even more applications of tapping, now using multiple fingers. You'll learn how to use these ideas in different genres and in alternate tunings. By the end of this book, you will be able to use tapping in many different musical contexts.

Tapping is a technique that can be useful in every guitarist's arsenal, no matter what kind of music you play. It should be viewed no differently than alternate picking, legato, or any other technique – it's simply a means to express yourself musically. I trust that you will discover new insights and ideas as you seek to improve your playing. Take the ideas that appeal to you and integrate them into your playing right away. I hope you'll be inspired to come up with your own ideas too. Remember, the music is at the fingertips of both your hands!

Kristof

Get the Audio

The audio files for this book are available to download for free from **www.fundamental-changes.com.** The link is in the top right-hand corner. Simply select this book title from the drop-down menu and follow the instructions to get the audio.

We recommend that you download the files directly to your computer, not to your tablet, and extract them there before adding them to your media library. You can then put them on your tablet, iPod or burn them to CD. On the download page there is a help PDF and we also provide technical support via the contact form.

For over 350 Free Guitar Lessons with Videos Check out:

www.fundamental-changes.com

Over 11,000 fans on Facebook: **FundamentalChangesInGuitar**

Instagram: **FundamentalChanges**

Get the Video

I've made multiple tuition videos to go with this book. Sometimes it's hard to capture the nuances of the music within the limitations of notation/tab. You can view the videos on the Fundamental Changes website here:

www.fundamental-changes.com/creative-tapping-videos

Chapter One: Tapping Fundamentals

In this chapter, we're going to begin with the absolute fundamentals of tapping. Starting simple, we'll look at which finger to use, how to dampen strings and how to develop control with both hands on the fretboard. If you're new to tapping, there's a lot to keep in mind, so make sure you watch the included videos at **www.fundamental-changes.com/creative-tapping-videos** for visual support and a more detailed explanation.

You should also download the audio for this book. When listening, you'll notice that most of the examples in this chapter are played both slow and fast. Practice with a metronome and always make sure you can play every example *cleanly* before increasing your speed.

Which finger is best?

Ultimately, choosing your main tapping finger is a personal decision, but here are some things for you to consider.

The index and middle fingers are by far the strongest and most commonly used fingers for tapping. If you frequently use a pick, it might not be advisable to use the index finger to tap, as the thumb and index finger are normally holding the pick. Personally, I find using the index finger makes it harder to switch fluently between picking and tapping, so it's become my habit to use the middle finger for tapping – even when playing just with my fingers – and you'll find that most of the licks in this book are easier to play this way.

Some players do use the index finger for tapping – such as Eddie Van Halen – in which case, the pick is temporarily held between the thumb and middle finger. The other option is to use the pick itself to tap, a technique made famous by Joe Satriani. (We will examine this approach in Chapter Two). While this makes a cool sound, I recommend that you learn the art of tapping with the fingers to begin with.

What is tapping?

You'll get into the technique of tapping much more easily if you think of it simply as playing hammer-ons and pull-offs that are executed with your picking hand. We're going to jump straight into some examples which are designed to help you develop control over the *hammer-ons*.

All tapped notes in this book are notated with a "T" above them. Here are some technique tips that will help you get the best sound:

• Always tap with the *tip* of your main tapping finger

• Tap your finger close to the fretwire, exactly where you'd position the fingers of your fretting hand

• Aim to tap cleanly and precisely on the string

• Use enough force so that the tapped note is as loud as if you'd picked it

Making the tapped notes loud enough is an essential part of achieving a convincing, authentic sound, and you'll need to work at this over time. At first, you may feel a bit of discomfort, as you'll need to build calluses on your fingertips. The fretting hand is used to this, but not so the picking hand.

Example 1a will help you to practice your tapping accuracy and work on the volume of the tapped notes. Tap across all six strings at the 12th fret. Move your fretting hand as necessary to silence any unwanted string noise. Focus on precision and tap close to the fretwire with the tip of your main tapping finger.

Example 1a

What makes tapping such a great effect is the sudden appearance of wide-interval lines that are not usually accessible through normal playing. However, you'll often need to pick a note then jump to another area of the fretboard to execute a tap. This means accuracy is key, but with time and patience you'll achieve the fluidity needed to make this technique sound great. When jumping across the fretboard, my advice is to *visualize* your destination and keep your movements as economical as possible.

This technique can be tricky when the distance to be covered by the picking hand is quite large and Example 1b will help you practice it. Fret the note on the D string, 7th fret with any finger. Now pick the string with a downstroke and move your picking hand to play the tapped note at the 12th fret. It always helps to find an anchor point, so the picking hand is in contact with the guitar at all times. In this case, rest your wrist lightly on the strings that are lower in pitch than the one you're playing. This will help you to maintain control and also dampen these strings.

It's really tempting to pick the string near to the 12th fret, instead of near the pickups as you would normally, but resist this for now. Picking notes directly above the fretboard doesn't produce the required tone and volume, and our aim here is to develop the ability of the picking hand to relocate and tap with accuracy. Practice this example on all strings to get used to the different feeling of each string and how much pressure must be applied to sound the note.

Example 1b

The next example flips things around to execute a pull-off. The idea here is to hold down the destination note with your fretting hand, tap on a higher fret, then pull away so that the fretted note sounds. Again, the aim is for both notes to sound with equal volume. To do this, don't just tap on the string and lift your tapping finger away from the fretboard, as this will result in one note being weaker in volume than the other.

Instead, you need to "flick" your finger away from the string. You can flick upwards or downwards, whichever you prefer, in a way that mimics picking the string. Try both approaches and see which works best for you. Personally, I choose to mimic a downstroke, as I find this allows me to dampen the other strings with more ease.

Example 1c

Now it's time to start building speed and accuracy by using your tapping finger for both hammer-ons and pull-offs. In Example 1d, hold down the note on fret 7 with any finger. Pick the string and hammer-on to the 12th fret with the picking hand, then immediately use the "flick" technique to execute a pull-off. This will be followed by another tap hammer-on and a pull-off, etc. There is only one pick stroke in this lick and after that, the sound is created entirely by your tapping finger. This exercise will help you develop your picking hand hammer-ons/pull-offs to achieve a consistent volume. Practice it across all the strings with a metronome.

Example 1d

String muting

When playing the previous examples, you probably noticed some unwanted string noise. Many guitarists have taken to using string dampeners to get rid of unwanted noise and such gadgets certainly help in recording sessions or gigs. For now, I suggest you don't use a dampener. You need to feel confident in your technical ability and forgoing a dampener will ensure your technique is developed to a level where one isn't a necessity. You'll then have the choice to use one in certain situations, but you'll know your tapping and muting techniques are flawless.

The image below indicates which parts of my hands I use to dampen the strings. In essence, it comes down to using as much of the flesh of both hands as possible to cancel out unwanted string noise.

The best way to think about muting is that each hand has a role to play.

The fretting hand (pictured on the left) mutes the strings higher in pitch than the one being played, by slightly arching the index finger. This means the index finger touches but doesn't sound the strings.

The picking hand (pictured on the right) mutes the strings lower in pitch than the string on which you're fretting a note. Here you have some options:

• As mentioned in Example 1b, you can find an anchor point for your picking hand, which will make it easier to execute all tapped notes. If you're holding a pick, rest your wrist lightly on the lower strings to mute them

• If you're not holding a pick, rest the thumb of the picking hand on the side of the fretboard. This anchor will give you control over your tapped notes, while simultaneously taking care of the unwanted string noise by touching the strings lightly with the joint of the thumb (the blue dot in the image).

Hammer-ons from nowhere with the fretting hand

The next fundamental component of tapping has been dubbed the "hammer-on from nowhere". This technique is performed solely by the fretting hand and doesn't involve any picking. In Example 1e, tap on fret 7 with your fretting hand index finger. Aim to hit the string close to the fretwire with the tip of the finger. Repeat this across all strings. Hammer-ons from nowhere are indicated by a "T" enclosed in a circle.

I tend to execute most hammer-ons from nowhere with the index finger, but it's a good exercise to practice using other fingers too. This will help to develop strength and accuracy in the fretting hand. Focus on tapping the strings precisely and remember to use both hands to dampen any unwanted string noise.

Example 1e

Combining tapping and hammer-ons from nowhere

The next example combines tapped strings and hammer-ons from nowhere. The repeating sequence begins with a picking hand tapped note at the 12th fret on the low E string, followed by a fretting hand hammer-on from nowhere at the 5th fret on the adjacent string. This pattern continues across the strings as shown in the notation.

In order to practice your accuracy/damping, take each bar in isolation to begin with before playing the whole lick. As ever, the main challenge will be to achieve a consistent volume and eliminate unwanted noise. Be sure to un-fret a note at the exact moment you play the next one, so they don't ring out at the same time. This means you need to lift up your main tapping finger at the precise moment you hammer-on from nowhere with the fretting hand and vice versa. Be sure to check out the video explanation for this technique as well.

Example 1f

So far, we've only been playing exercises, but the next example sounds more like a lick. Here, a hammer-on from nowhere is followed by a tap on the same string. The lick spells out the A Minor Pentatonic scale (A C D E G). The first note of the scale is hammered on, the second note tapped, the third hammered on etc. Because each tapped note is played an octave higher, we begin to hear the harp-like effect that tapping can produce.

Example 1g

Next up is an exercise that will further test your accuracy, as it calls for string skipping as well as hammer-ons from nowhere. You may notice more unwanted string noise when skipping strings, so your dampening technique will also be put to the test. The repeating pattern begins with a tapped 12th fret note on the low E string, followed by a hammer-on from nowhere on the D string.

Example 1h

Let's explore some more pentatonic scale exercises/licks. Example 1i utilizes both hands on the fretboard and brings together several of the techniques we've explored so far. It uses the common first position A Minor Pentatonic scale. To ascend the scale in bar 1, a combination of hammer-ons from nowhere and tapped notes is used. To descend the scale in bar 2 requires switching to the technique of fretting the lower note first, before executing a tap/pull-off from the higher note. This may be tricky at first but is a fantastic exercise to practice both technique and note separation.

Example 1i

The next example uses shape 2 of the A Minor Pentatonic scale and reverses the techniques of the previous example. This time, bar 1 is executed using tapped notes pulled off to fretted notes. Bar 2 is executed using hammer-ons from nowhere to tapped notes. Like the previous lick, the trickiest part here is switching techniques at the transition point from bar 1 to 2. Take things slowly at first to nail the technical aspects before increasing the tempo.

Example 1j

Example 1k is another "octave displacement" idea, where every second note is shifted up an octave. The technique creates big intervals to make things sound interesting and unpredictable.

Example 1k

The Chordal Capo

Now that you've practiced the fundamentals of tapping, it's time to use what you've learned in a more musical context. I like to call this technique the Chordal Capo. It involves holding down a chord shape and incorporating a lot of picking hand movement. It has lots of useful applications, like creating an atmospheric ending to a song.

The examples that follow are all executed in the same way:

•   Hold down the chord with the fretting hand (in this case the C Major barre chord on the 8th fret)

•   Execute a tapped pull-off across all strings at the 12th fret

The result is that all of the sound is created by the picking hand as it taps then pulls off to a note in the fretted chord. Here is how it sounds:

Example 1l

The next example shows a variation of the Chordal Capo technique. Let the notes of the chord ring out and experiment with moving this barre shape around the fretboard. Wherever you move it to, the tapped notes always go in a vertical line, four frets higher than the index finger of your fretting hand.

Example 1m

You can also hold down any of the CAGED chord shapes while you tap up and down the next pentatonic shape, as the next more challenging example shows. Play the C Major chord in the E shape, then the D shape, C shape, A shape and G shape. The chord shapes are indicated in the diagram below. For more information on the CAGED system, check out Joseph Alexander's book *The CAGED System and 100 Licks for Blues Guitar.*

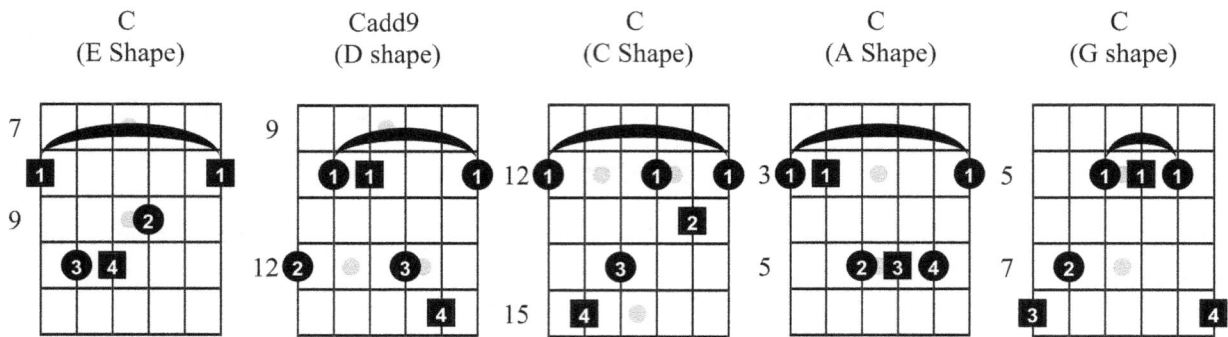

C (E Shape) Cadd9 (D shape) C (C Shape) C (A Shape) C (G shape)

Example 1n

In the next example you'll move the picking hand around the fretboard while the fretting hand holds down two chords – C Major then A minor. The exercise shows how you unlock new sounds by tapping in different areas of the fretboard, while still holding the same chord shape. As the picking hand moves around quite a bit, make sure you find an anchor point each time to keep the tapping accurate. Note that the change to the Am chord occurs halfway through bar 3.

Example 1o

It may have dawned on you that the possibilities of the Chordal Capo are limitless, so experiment on your own with variations of the licks above. You can also combine other techniques with tapped notes to create new sounds. Example 1p shows how you can add slides to this technique. This sounds more complicated than it is. You just need to mimic the motion your fretting hand makes when performing a slide. Here you need to tap the 5th fret on the A string, maintain the pressure on the string, and slide up to the 7th fret before flicking the tapping finger away to sound the fretted note at the 3rd fret. Repeat this motion on the other strings.

Example 1p

To close out this chapter, we're going to bring together everything you've learned thus far. Work your way through the following examples methodically and you'll have all the tools needed to perform the final piece of this chapter.

I suggest you practice these examples with and without a pick and be sure to focus on the distance the picking hand needs to cover to reach the tapped notes. The challenging part of the following examples is to judge how much pressure is needed to maintain the sound of the tapped notes when you slide. Take a close look at how your fretting hand executes a slide and mimic the motion exactly. You need to apply enough pressure to maintain the sound, while still being able to move your finger around.

Hold down the C Major barre chord and, after either picking or plucking the E, D, G and B strings, the tapping fun starts. Make sure you control the volume and timing of your slides and let every note ring out as much as possible. If you want some visual help with these examples, you can watch the video of the final piece of this chapter.

Example 1q

Example 1r uses exactly the same idea, but this time you pick an A minor chord and embellish it with lush tapped notes, hammer-ons and pull-offs.

Example 1r

Now do the same for the G Major barre chord in the next example.

Example 1s

Example 1t shows you the last two bars of the piece. This is a very musical approach that combines hammer-ons from the fretting hand with slides from the picking hand.

Example 1t

In this final example, you will hear how the Chordal Capo can be used as a compositional tool. The whole performance is based on the idea of holding down a chord and embellishing it with tapped notes. You've already practiced the building blocks of this piece, so all you need to do is to get the sound in your ears and start tapping. Have fun!

Example 1u

Congratulations! You are now familiar with the basic techniques required to tap. Here is a reminder of what to keep in mind:

• Tapping accuracy

• String dampening

• Note separation

• Consistent volume

• Timing

It's important to be realistic about how well you are playing the examples, so you might try recording yourself and studying the results. Is there any unwanted string noise? Are all the notes the same volume?

The next step is to transpose the patterns you've learnt to other keys. Practice this by taking one pattern and moving it up/down the fretboard. Make sure your practice is focused and use a metronome.

Once you are satisfied with the results, move on to the next chapter. Here you will learn to tackle some popular tapping licks, as well as learning some cool tapping tricks. Enjoy!

Chapter Two: Classic and Creative Tapping Licks

In this chapter you'll learn some tasty tapping licks to add to your vocabulary. By working your way through these examples, you'll notice progress straight away and soon be a master of tapping that axe.

First, we'll look at some classic tapping licks you need to know. They may be used frequently, but that's because they sound great. Since tapping is often used in Metal, if you kick on the overdrive/distortion, these licks will take you unmistakably in that direction.

Second, you'll remember that the aim of this book is to take tapping beyond the boundaries of Metal, so next I'll show you some examples to spice up your Pop, Rock, Blues or Country playing. There is a short solo at the end of this section that shows how you can implement these ideas in different genres.

The third section covers how to use tapping in more unconventional and creative ways, which is rewarding and a lot of fun. To end the chapter, the short piece "Flutter By" will teach you how to use the examples in another musical context. Be sure to listen to the audio files and check out the video performance at **www. fundamental-changes.com/creative-tapping-videos** for a deeper understanding of these examples.

Classic tapping licks

The first examples in this chapter will improve the coordination between your hands. They are single string exercises built around a D minor triad (D F A) and are great for working on your speed. Don't forget the lessons learned in Chapter One when playing the examples:

- Anchor the wrist of your picking hand on the lower strings to dampen them and be very precise with your tapping finger.

- Flick away with the tapping finger to make your pull-offs defined and make each note as long and loud as the next

It seems fitting to call these first few licks "tapping clichés" and it's important to work your way through them methodically as they will return in Example 2l in the form of a short solo.

Example 2a

In Example 2b, the same three notes are played in a different order. Focus on note separation, volume and timing. Try practicing in front of a mirror briefly to check that everything looks efficient but relaxed. Keep your forearm, wrist and hand in a relatively straight line, as this will make tapping feel more comfortable and natural without tiring your arm.

Example 2b

Let's increase the amount of work the fretting hand has to do by subdividing the notes into groups of four instead of three. This means the tapped note is followed by three notes played by the fretting hand.

Example 2c

Example 2d adds another string into this exercise. Focus on making the switch between strings as effortless as possible and watch out for any unwanted string noise. Since you're executing these first examples mainly on the high E and B strings, your picking hand is doing most of the string muting. Anchor your wrist in such a way that it covers all the strings except the ones you want to sound.

Example 2d

The next example is a pedal tone or pitch axis tapping cliché. You may recognize this from songs like *Satch Boogie* or *EVH*. Practice this example on all strings as it's a great way to get used to the different feel of each string.

Example 2e

You can also keep the ostinato (repeated note) in the picking hand, as shown in Example 2f. Here you play a D minor scale (D E F G A Bb C) up the D string, with tapped notes and open strings in between. Make sure you use the index finger of the fretting hand to dampen the G, B and high E strings, while the picking hand rests lightly on the low E and A strings.

Example 2f

Combining other techniques with tapping

Now let's add some slides to these tapping exercises to create a more slippery sound. When sliding, experiment to find the right amount of pressure to maintain the sound, while still being able to move around freely. In Example 2g, the idea is to tap the 17th fret on the B string, slide up to the 18th fret, then back down to the 17th fret before pulling-off.

Example 2g

Here is another tap and slide lick example in D minor, with added chromatic passing notes. Make sure you move a lick like this up/down the neck, to practice how far your picking hand needs to move for each key.

Example 2h

Another beautiful technique is to add a bend to a tapped note to create a bluesy sound. This is another idea that is much easier to execute than the notation suggests. Listen to the audio example and you'll quickly grasp the idea. In Example 2i, the bend is executed exclusively with the fretting hand. The only job the picking hand has is to tap the correct string/fret accurately – which is made a little harder than normal due to the strings being closer together.

Ideally, make the bend with the ring finger and allow your middle finger to move the other strings up a bit as well. This makes precise tapping easier. Watch the accompanying video for a demonstration.

Example 2i

The next example demonstrates a more advanced combination of bending and tapping. The frets indicated in the TAB show where you are to tap the fretboard, though the resulting note produced will sound a tone higher as you're bending the G string by a whole step.

Example 2j

Example 2k illustrates a technique famously used by the likes of John Mayer, which combines bends and slides in a tapping lick. The lick is based around the F Major Pentatonic scale (F G A C D) and you can break it into two parts and practice them separately.

In this first half of the lick, bend up from the 10th fret on the G string, tap the 13th fret, then release the bend and simultaneously slide down to the 12th fret with your tapping finger before you execute another bend, release and pull-off to finish the lick. In the second part you play the same lick an octave higher.

Example 2k

To end this section, there is a short solo for you to learn that combines all the techniques discussed in this chapter so far. You can play this over a Pop, Blues, Country, Rock or Metal track (depending on how much distortion you apply). There is an accompanying video for this piece, played slow and fast, so you can see exactly how to play it. It's made up of licks you've already played, so let's break it down:

- Bars 1 and 2 are based on examples 2i and 2j and use a combination of tapping and bending

- Bar 3 adds slides and uses ideas from examples 2a, 2b, 2c and 2d

- Bar 4 repeats the idea seen in Example 2k

- Bar 5 is a segue into bar 6, where Example 2g is repeated

- Bar 7 has a shortened ostinato tapping line, reminiscent of Example 2f

- To end the solo, play the lick with chromatic passing tones previously discussed in Example 2h

In the audio, you will hear the solo played four times, while the backing track changes between Blues, Pop, Country and Rock. As you can hear, tapping can sound really interesting over multiple styles of music.

Example 21

Tapping tricks

In this next part I will show you some new, creative and instantly usable tapping ideas. We'll utilise these ideas in the context of another solo at the end of the chapter.

At the end of Chapter One we looked at the Chordal Capo, executed by the fretting hand, but how about using the picking hand as the capo? This technique has been used by Paul Gilbert, Eddie Van Halen and others. The idea in Example 2m is to place one finger of the *picking hand* on the G string, 9th fret, as if a capo had been applied. I recommend using the tip of the middle finger, while the index and ring fingers mute the adjacent strings. Now, with your fretting hand tap a hammer-on from nowhere at the 16th fret before continuing with the rest of the lick. Use your ring finger or pinky to execute the first hammer-on from nowhere.

Example 2m

Let's take this idea a step further. Since you're not actually using a capo you have the freedom to move your picking hand "capo" around. This looks super flashy and will make your performances all the more entertaining to watch. Play this lick with attitude!

Example 2n

Here is another creative tapping technique that involves a different execution of a tapped note to create artificial or *tapped* harmonics. It requires what I'll call a *slap-tap*. Instead of tapping close to the fretwire, you tap *on the fretwire* itself – and for the shortest time possible, so you don't prevent the harmonic from ringing out.

Normally you will slap-tap twelve frets above the fretted note to create a note an octave higher, but this technique also works if you tap five frets or seven frets above the fretted note.

In Example 2o, the first bar is played by tapping the harmonic twelve frets above the fretted notes, and seven frets above in the second bar. This creates the sound of an octave up, and an octave plus a fifth up, and spells out the sound of Emaj7 and Bmaj7 chords. You may find it easier to sound the harmonics using the bridge pickup of your guitar.

Example 2o

Emaj7   Bmaj7

```
AH---------------------------------------------------------|
let ring---------------------------------------------------|
T|------------------4----5---|----------------4----5--------|
A|----------6----------------|----------6------------------ |
B|--7------------------------|--7--------------------------|
```

The next example is an exercise to help you get more comfortable executing the slap-tap. It's based on the E Major Pentatonic scale (E F# G# B C#) and the idea is to play each note followed by a tapped harmonic twelve frets higher. Your picking hand mirrors your fretting hand and plays the same scale twelve frets above your fretting hand, tapping each string's fretwire briefly and forcefully.

Example 2p

```
   AH AH AH AH AH AH AH AH    AH AH AH AH AH AH AH AH    AH AH AH AH AH AH AH
                                      7-7-9-9-9-9-7-7
                              7-7-9-9               9-9-7-7
T|                  6-6-9-9                                  9-9-6-6
A|          7-7-9-9         6-6-9-9                                    9-9-7-7
B|  7-7-9-9                                                                  9-9
```

Here's the same E Major Pentatonic scale shape, but instead of picking every note first, just play the tapped harmonic.

Example 2q

```
   AH-------------------------------------------------------------------------|
                                 7--9--9--7
T|                       7--9              9--7
A|                  6--9                         9--6
B|          6--9                                       9--6
   7--9                                                     9--7
                                                                 9--7--9
```

The two previous examples will serve as good exercises to practice this technique for accuracy and sound, but here's a more musical approach. You can use this technique more sparingly to emphasize certain notes. Example 2r is an E Major pentatonic phrase with tapped harmonics as accents, to really make the notes stand out. This lick will return in the piece at the end of this chapter, so make sure to listen to the audio example and spend some time to perfect it.

Example 2r

You can also use this technique on multiple notes and even chords. This will require excellent string dampening and you will need to angle your tapping finger to be perpendicular to the fretboard, to allow you to hit multiple strings simultaneously. I played this example fingerstyle and for the first time used my index finger rather than middle finger to execute the tapped notes. With a lick such as this, it's easier to get the right sound using the index finger to tap on multiple strings. The slap-tap will sound more musical if you don't use it on every note or chord, but rather as "seasoning" to emphasize certain moments in a progression.

Example 2s

Example 2t is another interesting way of combining tapping with harmonics to create a very unique sound. The idea is to tap the first note on each string, then pull off to a natural harmonic by lightly touching the string above the 7th fret with the index finger of the fretting hand, followed by a hammer-on with the ring finger or pinky of the fretting hand. This can be tricky to achieve at first, so go slowly and listen to the audio to hear what you're aiming for.

Example 2t

Let's move on to a new tapping trick that can create incredibly fast trills. In this technique, both hands take it in turns to tap the highest note of the trill. First the fretting hand executes a hammer-on followed by a pull-off, then the picking hand executes a tap followed by a pull-off. Thereafter they repeat the alternating pattern. In Example 2u, accuracy and coordination between the two hands should be your main focus, as this example could tie your fingers in a knot! Timing is less important here, just make sure you end on a strong beat after playing this insanely fast lick.

Example 2u

Example 2v is another fun exercise with a lot of musical applications – we'll call it the *tap 'n' slide*. Tap the first note with your picking hand, pull off, then instantly slide up to the same note with your fretting hand. Focus on the accuracy of the slid notes and experiment with where you start the slide. The slide just needs to be executed quickly, so it's really up to what sound you prefer.

Example 2v

To make things more interesting and musical, you can change up the notes as well. Play the following pentatonic run using the tap 'n' slide technique. (If you find it tricky, there's a video to help – the lick appears in bar 10 of the performance piece "Flutter By").

Example 2w

As an alternative to using the fingers of your picking hand to tap notes, you can use a pick, which sounds a little brighter and more aggressive. Joe Satriani has used this to create a cool trill effect by tapping really fast. To get the right sound, hold the pick between the thumb and index finger of your picking hand and rotate it, so that it hits the string/fret at a 90-degree angle. If you want to experiment with this technique some more, go back and apply it to some of the earlier examples in the book.

Example 2x

Example 2y is an interesting way of playing one line with the picking hand and another with the fretting hand, an idea we will develop further in Chapter Five. When you tap on fret 21 on the B string, make sure you hold this note (add vibrato for better sustain) while you trill between the 14th and 16th frets on the D string with your fretting hand. Both strings should be audible, which means your trill will have to be executed quite softly compared to the tapped note.

Example 2y

The next two examples change things up again and use a slide or bottleneck in combination with tapping. Thinking out of the box often requires us to adapt things we know in a new way and this is a perfect illustration. Example 2z is played with a weak slap-tap. Gently touch the note twelve frets above the note played with your slide, then slide up one octave the where you originally touched the note. This creates an amazing sound that is used by the likes of Ariel Posen, Joey Landreth and Derek Trucks.

Example 2z

I urge you to check out the guitarists mentioned in this book, but in particular Ron "Bumblefoot" Thal. His terrifying approach to tapping is an amazing source of inspiration (after the initial shock and disbelief you will experience witnessing such ludicrous speed and power!) In Example 2za you will no longer be limited by the number of frets you have. Instead, by using a slide you will be able to access and tap notes that are even higher than the highest note on your fingerboard. The idea is to tap with the slide where the note would be, so it's important to trust your ears for this exercise. Rather than a slide, Ron Thal uses an iron thimble on the pinky of his picking hand to execute the high notes. If you can find one, feel free to use this instead of a slide!

Example 2za

To end this chapter, here is the performance piece referred to earlier. It contains many of the techniques you've learnt so far. You'll use the bending/tapping and slap-tap tricks from examples 2u and 2v. It also incorporates the technique of using two hands to play different lines, like Example 2y. The ending is a combination of Example 2t and a Chordal Capo lick.

Be sure to watch the included video at **www.fundamental-changes.com/creative-tapping-videos** where I play this piece both fast and slow. This video will help you along the way, but if you've worked your way through this chapter you can already play most of the licks, so have fun!

2zb "Flutter By" performance piece

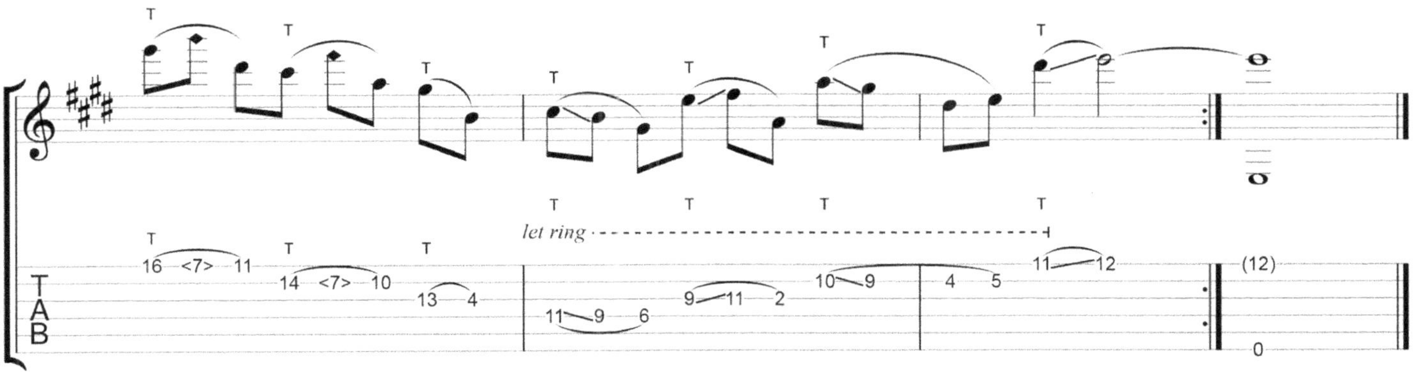
T
let ring
TAB

Chapter Three: Tapping Arpeggios and Pentatonic Licks

In the previous chapters we've focused on polishing tapping technique and learning some tasty licks to add to your vocabulary. In this chapter, it's back to the woodshed to see how to apply what you've learnt to a range of arpeggios across the fretboard. The aim here is to increase your fretboard visualization and fluency, and help you apply the technique of tapping more broadly.

First, you'll learn how to arpeggiate minor, major, diminished, sus2 and sus4 chords and their inversions. After learning these arpeggios on one string, you'll then learn how to arpeggiate the same chords in multiple octaves on two and even three strings. The next step is to extend these triad shapes to become 7th chord arpeggios. Next, you'll apply these arpeggios on multiple strings incorporating hammer-ons from nowhere. Finally, you'll discover some less common arpeggio shapes and, by the end of the chapter, be playing some advanced pentatonic tapping licks.

We'll take a linear approach to playing these arpeggios, because this lends itself very well to tapping. While examples like 3a below, which features sweep picking and tapping, are arguably a lot of fun to play, they won't be heavily featured. That said, I don't want to keep this one arpeggio tapping cliché from you! Play this one by picking through the notes with all downstrokes. For the phrase on the high E string, use hammer-ons and pull-offs and tap the note at the 15th fret with your middle finger, before sweeping back through the arpeggio.

Example 3a

Triad arpeggios on one string

Let's start this section with a G Major arpeggio (G B D) played in all three inversions. The first phrase begins on the G root note, the second phrase on the B (3rd), and the third phrase on the D (5th). Each phrase begins with a hammer-on from nowhere. Play the hammer-ons with the pinky or ring finger.

This is the kind of exercise you can easily transfer to other strings to get used to how they feel. The shape will be the same for all major chords, so once you know which note to begin on, you can arpeggiate them all over the neck.

Example 3b

To play a G minor arpeggio, all you have to do is lower the third by one fret. The notes are now G, Bb and D. Example 3c shows how to play the G minor triad through its three inversions. Spend a moment to get used to the difference in intervals between the major and minor arpeggios. Execute this example the same way as the previous one, playing two notes with the fretting hand and one with the picking hand.

Example 3c

If we also lower the fifth, we get a G diminished arpeggio (G Bb Db). Now, all three notes are a minor third (three frets) apart. With some of these inversions, there are wide stretches involved. If the stretch feels at all uncomfortable, feel free to move the whole shape up the fretboard where the frets are closer together.

Example 3d

Armed with the major, minor and diminished triad shapes you've just learned, it's possible to play through all the diatonic triads in a key. Example 3e demonstrates the triads in the G Major Scale (G A B C D E F#). You will play consecutively through the triads G, Am, Bm, C, D, Em and F#dim in their root positions. You can use the TAB/notation of the previous examples to figure out how to play the inversions of each triad too!

Example 3e

Sus-chords are an interesting way to break away from the predictability of major and minor arpeggios. In a sus chord, the third is swapped or *suspended*. Example 3f shows you the three inversions of Gsus2 (G A D).

Example 3f

Another possibility is the Gsus4 chord (G C D).

Example 3g

Triad arpeggios on multiple strings

When you have worked through the previous examples and feel comfortable tapping arpeggios on a single string, it's time to incorporate the same ideas on multiple strings and in multiple octaves. So that you explore other areas of the fretboard, we move into the key of C Major. Example 3h demonstrates a tapped C Major arpeggio (C E G) followed by a D minor arpeggio (D F A), both in root position.

As you begin to do more string skipping, make sure your dampening of unwanted string noise is on point. This example is notated twice, as there are two ways to play it. The idea is to execute these shapes by playing two notes with the fretting hand and one with the picking hand on each string. Since you've practiced hammer-ons from nowhere a lot, it's time to consider an alternative way to play the next string. If you tap with the middle finger of your picking hand, you have the option to pluck the first note on each new string with your ring finger. If your index finger is your main tapping finger, you can pluck the next string with your middle finger. This approach will help you to create a continuous and fluent sound when changing to the next string. Plus, it will give you even more control over the volume. Be sure to use this technique to execute the following examples, as well as playing them with hammer-ons from nowhere.

Example 3h

For Example 3i we move back to a G Major chord, followed by an A minor chord (A C E), both in first inversion (beginning on the 3rd of the chord). Other than dampening unwanted string noise, make sure your notes aren't ringing out at the same time. Un-fret each note exactly when you fret the next one and make the volume very consistent. The transition to the next string is probably the hardest part of these examples, so split up each exercise into smaller bits and practice them individually before connecting them together.

Make a judgement on how good your string dampening, hammer-ons from nowhere and un-fretting of the notes is. Ask yourself if it sounds the way you want it to. By practicing like this, you will work methodically to increase your control over the notes.

Example 3i

The next example is another G Major arpeggio followed by an A minor arpeggio, but now in second inversion (beginning on the 5th).

Example 3j

Example 3k is a combination of different inversions on multiple strings. This is an interesting way to play a G Major arpeggio all over the neck, from the lowest note to the highest.

Example 3k

The options here are limitless. For the sake of continuity, I urge you to spend some time working out diminished and sus-chord arpeggios on multiple strings as well. The whole system is very logical: you continue to play two notes with the fretting hand, followed by one tapped note. Now, however, we're moving on to arpeggios containing four notes instead of three.

7th chord arpeggios on one string

As 7th chords have an extra note, it means there's also an extra inversion. There are many different ways of playing the following examples but in order to avoid insanely wide stretches, you will start with a hammer-on from nowhere with the fretting hand index finger. This is followed by a hammer-on with either the ring finger or pinky before tapping and sliding with your tapping finger. Example 3l is a Gmaj7 chord (G B D F#) and its inversions.

Example 3l

In the examples that follow, we'll work through other chord types as we did earlier, all with G as the root to help you learn the different intervals required to play major, dominant, minor, half diminished and diminished chord arpeggios.

When we shift the major 7th interval of the chord down by a semitone we get a G Dominant 7 or G7 arpeggio (G B D F).

Example 3m

Once you're comfortable with the G7 shape, you can move it around the fretboard to play a 12-bar blues progression. You wouldn't necessarily play something like this over a blues, but since the sequence is so familiar, it's a great way to practice relocating the shape. To change things up a bit, we'll move from the low E string and begin this on the D string. To limit your hand movements, play the inversions of each chord that are closest together, as shown in the notation.

Example 3n

You may have guessed that the minor 7 arpeggio is next! Lower the 3rd of the Gmaj7 chord by a semitone and it results in a Gm7 chord (G Bb D F).

Example 3o

For the next chord the 5th gets flattened as well, which produces a Gmin7b5 chord (or G half diminished – G Bb Db F). Take a moment to think through the logic behind these arpeggios: we began with Gmaj7 and by constantly changing one note, we can find all of the diatonic 7th chord arpeggios.

Example 3p

Example 3q takes you through each of the diatonic 7th chords in the G Major scale in root position. For homework, you can figure out the inversions of each chord on your own.

Example 3q

G Diminished 7 (G Bb Db Fb) is a useful arpeggio shape to work with, as all of the notes are the same distance (three frets) apart. This means you can play all of the inversions in exactly the same way and they fall nicely under the fingers.

Example 3r

7th chord arpeggios on multiple strings

From this point onwards, you will learn more interesting and creative ways to play arpeggios all over the neck. Multiple key signatures will be covered to push you further out of your comfort zone, but the shapes of the arpeggios will be the same as the previous examples. Hammer-ons from nowhere and string muting are crucial to perfectly execute the following licks.

Each example will focus on one aspect that will increase your fretboard visualization, finger independence and fluency. Should this be too easy for you, you can always extrapolate the ideas and use them for other 7th chords and inversions. This section is less strict and structured than the previous sections, so let's get to it!

Example 3s shows you two ways to play a Gmaj7 arpeggio in first inversion and two ways to play it in third inversion. While learning these inversions on multiple strings, it may be more comfortable to play three notes with the fretting hand and only one with the picking hand. Try this and the previous method (two notes each between the fretting and picking hands) and see which works best for you.

Example 3s

Bars 1 and 2 of Example 3t show how to play an Amin7 arpeggio (A C E G) on two strings. This sequence gets repeated an octave higher in bars 3 and 4. Practice these phrases separately before tackling the whole example. Sequences like this can be very useful – you don't always need to cover the whole range of the fretboard. Remember that instead of using hammer-ons from nowhere, you have the option to pluck the first note on each new string.

Example 3t

Rather than playing each arpeggio up and down, it can be more interesting and unpredictable to switch up the order of the notes. In the next example, a D7 arpeggio (D F# A C) is played rather freely, so make sure you listen to the audio to hear how this exercise sounds before tackling it.

Example 3u

Let's tap through the popular I IV V I chord progression (Cmaj7 – Fmaj7 – G7 – Cmaj7) using multiple octaves. Make sure you break this example up into smaller fragments to practice before putting it all together, as there's a lot going on here. The idea of this lick is to always switch to the closest note of the next arpeggio. Listen to the audio a couple of times to hear how it should sound. In the last bar, to sound the C chord, hold the 19th fret on the A string with your tapping finger, while performing two hammer-ons from nowhere, with the ring and index fingers of the fretting hand respectively.

Example 3v

If we take a less linear approach to playing arpeggios, we can find some useful shapes that fall easily under the fingers, such as Example 3w.

This exercise is split into four parts, each comprising two bars. Bars 1-2 show how to play a Cmaj7 arpeggio (C E G B) by alternating the two hands – a hammer-on from nowhere is followed by a tapped note, and this pattern repeats. Bars 3-4 have another Cmaj7 arpeggio, but this time each note is played on a new string. The key to clarity here is to un-fret each note exactly as you fret the next one.

Bars 5-8 repeat this idea with a Dmin7 arpeggio (D F A C). Even though it may appear easier to just play hammer-ons with the fretting hand, be sure you also execute the Dmin7 arpeggios by alternating hands.

Example 3w

We can find even more ways to play the same arpeggios. Example 3x takes the middle path between the linear and non-linear approaches we've discussed. The result is a fluid sound, achieved by a repeating pattern of a single note on one string, followed by three notes on the next string (bars 1-4). The pattern is reversed for bars 5-8 with three notes per string followed by a single note, etc.

Example 3x

Other interesting arpeggios

Leaving certain notes out of a chord in favor of others is an excellent way to create great sounding shapes that are easier to execute. The next example has a very versatile shape that can be tweaked to produce either a major or minor sound.

Bars 1-2 of this lick can be viewed as Gadd9 arpeggio (G A B D). Notice that you only tap one note of each phrase with the picking hand here. Playing notes with the fretting hand is something you've been doing since you first picked up the guitar, so it makes sense to use this to your advantage. The Gadd9 arpeggio is followed by an Em(add13) arpeggio (E G A B), which is achieved by changing just one note.

Example 3y

Example 3z is another popular chord progression (IV V I I) and is entirely based on the shape of the Gadd9 arpeggio from the previous example. Again, the idea here is to always change to the closest chord tone of the next arpeggio, which will increase your ability to use different inversions more freely on the fretboard. Be sure to listen to the audio for this example, as it sounds a bit unpredictable at first. Once your ears get used to the sound, it'll be easier to play.

Example 3z

Advanced pentatonic tapping licks

We'll close out this chapter by adding one more note to our arpeggios. However, instead of thinking about this in a chordal way, it'll be easier to get your head around them if you view them as advanced pentatonic tapping licks. Here, I want to show you one of my favorite tapping approaches and I'm sure it'll give you new ideas to add to your (by now) already quite extensive tapping vocabulary.

The remainder of the examples in this chapter all use a three-note-per-string approach and employ quite a lot of string skipping.

The sequence to this first lick is a hammer-on from nowhere, followed by a regular fretting hand hammer-on, followed by a picking hand tap when ascending. When descending, the pattern is a picking hand tap which pulls off to a fretted note, then a fretting hand pull-off which sounds the last fretted note in each group.

Example 3za

```
T      T  T       T       T          T          T          T
e|--------------------------------------------------------------------|
B|--------------------------------------------------------------------|
G|-----------------------5--8--10--8--5-------------------------------|
D|----------5--7--10-------------------------10--7--5-----------------|
A|-5--8--10----------------------------------------------10--8----5---|
E|--------------------------------------------------------------------|
```

Example 1m is the same idea moved across to begin on the A string.

Example 3zb

```
T      T  T       T       T          T          T
e|--------------------------------------------------------------------|
B|--------------------------------------------------------------------|
G|-----------------------5--8--10--8--5-------------------------------|
D|----------5--7--9--------------------------9--7--5------------------|
A|-5--7--10----------------------------------------------10--7----5---|
E|--------------------------------------------------------------------|
```

It is important to get used to all the pentatonic boxes, so the following example shows you a combination of positions two and three of the A Minor Pentatonic scale.

Example 3zc

```
T       T  T       T       T          T          T
e|--------------------------------------------------------------------|
B|--------------------------------------------------------------------|
G|------------------------8--10--13--10--8----------------------------|
D|-----------7--10--12------------------------12--10--7---------------|
A|-8--10--12------------------------------------------------12--10----8--|
E|--------------------------------------------------------------------|
```

A fun way to create more unique sounding licks is to skip notes in the scale, rather than playing them in sequence.

Example 3zd

The same pattern applied to the A, G and high E strings sounds like this.

Example 3ze

We conclude this chapter with an in-depth study that illustrates all the positions of the A Minor Pentatonic scale in useful three-note-per-string patterns. It also incorporates the string skipping idea we've been working on. Be sure to split this exercise up into smaller fragments to figure out which positions you like to use best. This is a good exercise to make a part of your regular practice routine.

Example 3zf

As you can see, there's a lot you can do just with tapped arpeggios, but it's time to move on. Transfer the ideas you've learnt to other keys, other string sets, or even try reversing the patterns. Exhaust the possibilities and hold onto the sounds you like. The main aim is to continue to increase your fretboard visualization, chord knowledge, and finger independence and fluency.

Chapter Four: Introducing More Fingers of The Picking Hand

Which fingers are best?

Now that you feel comfortable using both hands on the fretboard, it's time to get a little crazier and include more fingers of the picking hand. To help you choose your second tapping finger here are some tips: if you use your index finger as your main tapping finger, I suggest you include your middle finger next, since there is a lot of strength and flexibility in this finger combination. You can also use your ring finger as your second tapping finger if a bigger stretch is required.

For guitarists like me, who frequently use a pick and tap mainly with the middle finger of their picking hand, it's easiest to include the ring finger as your second tapping finger. In this scenario, you can just keep holding the pick, while performing gymnastics on the fretboard with both hands. However, while there are definite benefits to this approach, it also has its limitations. For instance, it's quite difficult to tap a note with the ring finger that's lower than the one tapped with the middle finger.

Example 4a calls for two picking hand fingers to be used simultaneously. This exercise instantly shows that my preferred combination of middle and ring fingers sometimes has its limitations. In this first example, a combination of index and middle fingers is the best solution. If you're holding a pick, tuck it into the palm of your hand and hold it there with the ring and pinky fingers, or hold it with your lips! Watch the included video at **www.fundamental-changes.com/creative-tapping-videos** for a detailed explanation of how best to tuck away your pick.

Example 4a

The next examples are reminiscent of the first examples in Chapter Two.

Example 4b

The next lick is the same as Example 2d, which you executed by tapping with one finger. See if you can increase the speed by assigning a different finger of the picking hand to each string.

Example 4c

In Example 4d, play both strings simultaneously to create the sound of double-stops.

Example 4d

By now, you've probably noticed that different licks will have a different ideal secondary tapping finger. This should motivate you to train all the fingers of your picking hand, so you can choose which finger to use at will. Putting this work in will also improve your tapping accuracy and control.

It's important to build up the calluses now, so I urge you to go back to some of the examples in previous chapters and practice them exclusively with other fingers of your picking hand. For example, repeat the 7th chord arpeggios from Chapter Three and play the two highest notes on each string with your main tapping finger and secondary tapping finger respectively, instead of sliding.

The Chordal Capo revisited

Now we're going to revisit the Chordal Capo technique from Chapter One. The next examples will show you more ways to use it, while you get used to tapping with multiple fingers of the picking hand. I played all of the following examples with the middle and ring fingers of my picking hand unless otherwise indicated.

For Example 4e, hold down a G Major chord with the E shape with the fretting hand, and tap two strings simultaneously across the 7th fret. Let every note ring out as much as possible and remember that all of the sound is created by the picking hand.

Example 4e

You can use this idea on two consecutive strings instead of leaving a gap. In the next example, hold down a G Major chord with the C shape, tap across the 12th fret and pull-off two strings at the same time to ring out the fretted chord.

Example 4f

So far, you've used the Chordal Capo to enhance one chord, but you can use it to play through whole chord progressions too. For Example 4g, you stay in one position on the fretboard. Notice that the tapping pattern changes in bar 2, where you tap the 8th fret on the B string with your second tapping finger. Every other time you tap the 7th fret across all strings.

Example 4g

In Example 4h you fret the G Major chord with the E shape, while you execute double stops on the D and B strings with the index and middle fingers of the picking hand. To end this example, hit all of the strings across the 15th fret with the whole length of the index finger of your picking hand. The *slap-tap* discussed in Chapter Two will create the artificial harmonics of most of the notes of the G Major chord.

Example 4h

The last bar of the next example adds hammer-ons with the fretting hand to the Chordal Capo. These double-stop ideas are great to include in songs. Here too, it makes sense to use the index and middle fingers of the picking hand to execute the tapped notes.

Example 4i

Pentatonic licks using multiple fingers from the picking hand

In the next example, the distance between your main tapping finger and secondary tapping finger is quite large, so it might be beneficial to use two non-neighboring fingers of the picking hand. Legends like Mr Guthrie Govan use their middle finger and pinky to tap wider intervals like these, but other options include the combination of the index and ring fingers, or even the index and the pinky. I still prefer to use my middle and ring fingers, but it's quite a stretch.

For consistency, all of the examples in this section are based around the A Minor Pentatonic scale (A C D E G). In Example 4j, the picking hand mirrors what the fretting hand plays one octave higher when ascending. When descending, the fretting hand mirrors the notes that the picking hand taps.

Example 4j

In the next example, the use of double-stops requires you to change the fingering of the picking hand quite a bit. We've talked about multiple finger combinations and for this exercise, I recommend you use the index and middle fingers of the picking hand. Here too, the fretting and picking hands mirror each other and play the same notes an octave apart.

Example 4k

The slap-tap can also be executed with two fingers of the fretting hand. For the next and following examples, I suggest you revert back to my favorite finger combination of middle and ring fingers to tap.

Example 4l

A linear approach to the pentatonic scale can make you sound very slick, as demonstrated in the example below. This idea effectively combines positions 1 to 3 of the A Minor Pentatonic scale and this four-note-per-string approach splits the workload between the two hands evenly. Each hand plays two of the notes per string.

Example 4m

When you combine the four-note-per-string approach from the previous example with string skipping, you can run through the scale very smoothly. Here is a more complex idea, so be sure to split it up into smaller two-bar sections to learn it.

Example 4n

Instead of playing the scale up and down, you can create some variation by playing a sequence on all six strings. This means you start off with a four-note-per-string pentatonic pattern on the low E and D strings that repeats on the A and G strings, and so on. As another variation, you can also practice this lick back to front.

Example 4o

The shapes in the previous examples can sound quite predictable, so let's change things up a bit. In Example 4p there are no three-fret-stretches in the picking, which means this shape falls much easier under the fingers.

Example 4p

Arpeggio ideas using multiple fingers from the picking hand

As previously mentioned, it's important to go back through the previous licks and execute them using other fingers to tap. The next three examples illustrate a different way of tackling ideas similar to those we've already explored, based around Amaj7 and Bm7 arpeggios.

Achieving a consistent volume becomes more of a challenge when you add a second finger to your tapping lines, so be aware of this. In Example 4q, each note is played on a different string, with the workload split evenly between the two hands. Start by hammering-on from nowhere with two fingers of the fretting hand, followed by tapping two notes with the picking hand, then repeat this pattern throughout. The easiest way to execute this example is by using the index and middle fingers of the picking hand to tap the notes.

Example 4q

Example 4r is very similar to the previous exercise but the order of the notes has changed, which makes it easier to use the middle and ring fingers of the picking hand as your main and secondary tapping fingers.

Example 4r

Here is another example where a linear approach is used to play both arpeggios in their first inversions. My preference is to use the middle and ring fingers of my picking hand to tap.

Example 4s

Now that you're training multiple fingers of the picking hand, it's important to realize that there are almost always multiple ways to play something. In the next example, I've notated a Bm(add9) arpeggio (B D F# C#) in eight different ways by using different string combinations and splitting the workload between the two hands in different ways.

Explore this idea and decide whether you favor your fretting hand doing most of the work, your tapping hand, or an even split. They are all viable options, so figure out what works best for you. This is perhaps one of the most useful exercises in the whole book, so spend some time practicing each bar on its own before you move on to the next one.

In bar 1, all of the notes are executed with the fretting hand, and in bar 2, one finger of the picking hand is introduced. Bar 3 uses both main and secondary tapping fingers before including slides in bars 4 and 5. In bar 6, you use more than two fingers from the picking hand for the first time. I suggest using index, middle and ring, but it would be equally valid to use your middle, ring and pinky. Bars 7 and 8 focus more on string skipping and alternative places on the fretboard to play the same arpeggio.

Example 4t

To finish this section, here is a simple chord progression played in two different ways. Test it out to see which way you prefer. Take a moment to think about how you want these arpeggios to sound: do you prefer to let the notes ring out or do you favor the sound of staccato (short) notes? This example has a lot of stacked fifths, an approach used in many hit songs by artists ranging from The Police to Jeff Beck.

Example 4u

A scalar approach

So far, we haven't spent much time exploring the major scale, but now we'll look at a few major licks. The focus of the following examples is a four-note-per-string way of playing the major scale and its modes. You will play these licks with two fingers of your fretting hand and two of your picking hand – an approach heavily used by guitarist Don Lappin. You've already used this 2 + 2 idea in some of the previous arpeggios but the applications are enormous.

The next example has a G Major scale (G A B C D E F#) played up and down one octave. The combination of middle and ring fingers works well for this approach, but experiment using index and middle, index and ring or even middle and pinky.

Example 4v

You can also play the previous example in multiple octaves, as notated below. Example 4w takes a structured approach: there are three different shapes and each one is played on two consecutive strings. There shouldn't be an audible difference between notes played with the fretting hand and notes played with the picking hand, so I suggest you focus on your hammer-ons from nowhere. It can get tricky to pluck the next string with another finger of the picking hand when using multiple fingers to tap, but aim to make all of the notes equally long and practice this lick in reverse as well.

66

Use the same 2 + 2 idea to play A Dorian (A B C D E F# G), the second mode of the G Major scale, and notice how the shapes discussed in the previous example are roughly the same for all of the modes.

Example 4x

When you start switching up the order of the notes, the music you play becomes less predictable, as shown in example 4y. This is based on a C Lydian Scale (C D E F# G A B), the fourth mode of the G Major Scale and make sure you listen to the audio example to get used to the sound. I suggest you put your pick down for this example, as I use the middle and ring fingers of the picking hand to play all of the tapped notes, except in the last bar, where I favor my index and middle fingers to tap and hold the chord.

Example 4y

Now let's switch from the 2 + 2 to a 3 + 1 approach. This means you will be using three fingers from the fretting hand and only one from the picking hand to execute Example 4z, which is one of my favorite slippery sounding licks. To get you more comfortable on every area of the fretboard the next three licks are based in E Major (E F# G# A B C# D#).

Example 4z

The previous example shows that there are often multiple ways to execute certain exercises. The next two examples require you to use the 2 + 2 idea in a less linear way, which instantly brings the shape from Guthrie Govan's song *Sevens* to mind. Example 4za is a fun variation on his lick and for a clear execution, make sure the notes don't ring at the same time. Un-fret one note at the exact moment you play the next one and focus on volume and timing. Every note is played on a new string, which creates a very unique rhythmic sound.

Example 4za

To end this chapter, here's a more sequential way to use the idea from the previous example.

Example 4zb

In this chapter, you've worked on all of the essential components of tapping with multiple fingers: strength, accuracy, dampening, timing, note separation and volume. This should have helped you to become comfortable using multiple fingers of both hands on the fretboard freely, so it's time to look at more musical ways to incorporate this technique into your playing.

Chapter Five: Using Tapping Tastefully

In this chapter we will begin to bring together everything you've learned and add some new licks along the way. The purpose of this chapter is to take the knowledge and techniques you've developed and apply them in tasteful, creative ways. You can add tapping to your playing in whatever way you feel, but make sure you use your powers for good! Use tapping to express, not to impress.

To build on what you've learnt, the examples in this chapter are in lots of different key signatures, to get you used to tapping all over the fretboard. Generally, the pieces are also longer and some of them use tapping more sparingly, so you can see how tapping may be tastefully incorporated to add spice to a performance.

This chapter is intended to release your musicality and creativity, so enjoy! Also be sure to check out the video at **www.fundamental-changes.com/creative-tapping-videos**, as I've recorded fast and slow versions for many of the examples in this chapter.

Emulating other instruments

It's possible to evoke the sounds of other instruments with tapping and there are several approaches you can take. We'll start by mimicking the sound of a *blues harp* on the guitar. This first example can be performed with or without a slide, so the lick is notated for each method.

First up is the slide part: slide up to the 12th fret on the B string, tap the 15th fret repeatedly and slide down and back up into the 12th fret. When you play this lick without the use of a slide, it's easiest to achieve a similar sound by using bends.

Example 5a

One of my favorite instruments is the *pedal steel* and it's possible to achieve this kind of sound with tapping. The idea is to use the fretting hand to bend behind the tapped notes. Here the focus must be on the accuracy and speed of your bends. You want the notes to reach their correct pitch quickly, similar to the way a pedal steel player would execute this. Bend the B string with the ring finger and the G string with the middle finger of your fretting hand behind the tapped notes. Remember to be very precise with your main tapping finger.

Example 5b

Example 5c is a more advanced lick that emulates the pedal steel. Do listen to the audio example for a better understanding of how to get it sounding exactly right. The techniques required are the same as in the previous example, but here all of the bends are executed with the ring finger of your fretting hand. This example outlines a chord progression in A Major going between E, D and A.

Example 5c

The next two examples demonstrate pianistic chord voicings that are almost impossible to play on guitar unless you incorporate tapping. Plucking all of the strings is quite tricky here, so instead you can strum everything with the spare fingers of your picking hand, while this hand is also holding down a tapped note. You can choose how dense you make these piano voicings – you don't have to play all of the strings, as is shown in the first two bars of the example below.

Example 5d

Badd9add11   Aadd9add#11   Emaj7   C#m11/B   B11/A   Emaj7

v

Another way to play voicings like these is to play hammer-ons from nowhere on multiple strings with the fretting hand while simultaneously executing a tapped note on the A string with the picking hand. This sounds more like how a piano player would play it. Be sure to focus on getting the same volume for all of the notes.

Example 5e

Alternate tunings

You can also apply tapping techniques to altered tunings to produce new, creative sounds. The following examples are given just to start you off with alternate tunings and the key word is *experiment*. This is a big area for exploration, and is an inexhaustible source of creativity, as you can always come up with different tunings. This approach is especially popular among acoustic guitar players like Andy McKee and in Math Rock with bands like American Football and CHON.

An entire book could be written on this topic, but here are some examples to get you started. We won't look at baritone tuning (B E A D F# B), drop D or drop C tunings here, as they are very closely related to standard tuning.

As a visual aid, it can be beneficial to get a fretboard diagram and write down the notes of each tuning. You will come up with shapes that are impossible to play in standard tuning as you discover new tools to compose original music, so it's good to have a road map.

Example 5f is written in open C tuning (C G C G C E), a tuning often used by John Butler. While it spells out a C Major chord, you can also experiment with C minor by detuning your high E string to Eb. In this piece, your picking hand covers all of the notes on the low C string, while all the other notes are played by hammering-on from nowhere with the fretting hand. Once you're used to this tuning, check out the "Nick Drake" tuning as well (C G C F C E) – it only has one note different to open C.

Example 5f

Slap-tapped or tapped harmonics sound great in open D tuning (D A D F# A D) and open E (identical to open D with every string tuned up a tone). In bars 1 and 2, hit the 12th fret so that the natural harmonics sound a D chord.

Example 5g

DADGAD tuning has long been popular in Folk music and a lot of acoustic guitar players use this tuning as well. The following example is inspired by the great Nathaniel Murphy, who's technical ability seems limitless, so be sure to check him out on Instagram @zeppelinbarnatra. Aim to play this as tightly as possible.

Example 5h

One of the most inspiring things is to create your own tunings, for instance by tuning the strings to the notes of your favorite chord. In the next example, the guitar is tuned to C# A A E A D, which spells out an Aadd11/C# chord.

Example 5i

F A C G B E is a tuning often used by Yvette Young, an incredibly unique musician with a very original approach to the instrument. Be aware that the following example changes time signatures, which is quite common in Math Rock. On top of that there are a lot of fingers from both hands involved, so this example is easiest to play without holding a pick. It's almost like playing piano on a guitar, with each hand doing its own thing.

Example 5j

If you want to experiment with other tunings, a good place to start is to take one of the tunings we've discussed and change one or more strings. Here are some others you might like to try:

C D G A E G: New Standard Tuning (Robert Fripp)

D A D G B D: Double Drop D Tuning

D G D G B D: Open G Tuning

D A D F# A E: Dadd9 Tuning

E G# B F# B D#: Emaj9 Tuning

There could be so many more, so experiment away!

In the previous section we touched on examples from Folk music and Math Rock and now we'll explore a number of other genres where tapping can be incorporated. One important thing to realize is that while the following licks are demonstrated in a specific genre, you can adapt them to any genre and a multitude of musical settings.

In the following examples you will often need to let you picking hand "float" above the fretboard to let everything ring out, so place your forearm on the guitar as an anchor point.

The idea in Example 5k is based on Sammy Boller's unique playing style, which incorporates a lot of tapping. Play the root and the fifth of each chord with the fretting hand using hammer-ons from nowhere, while executing the melody with the picking hand. It's quite an intuitive approach and you can create a lot of beautiful Ambient music with this type of playing.

Example 5k

Next up is an example based on the same three chords, but now you use multiple fingers of the picking hand to tap.

Example 5l

Example 5m is based on a genre not often associated with tapping – the 12-bar blues. To play this, the fretting hand takes care of the bass notes, while the picking hand taps the other notes of the chords. Because both hands have a lot to do here, the notation is quite dense, so be sure to watch the included video material to get a better grasp of how this is supposed to sound.

Example 5m

If you haven't done so already, check out the legendary Stanley Jordan, who's use of tapping has given him an incredibly unique voice on the instrument. He has created guitar arrangements of classic tunes such as *Stairway to Heaven* and *Eleanor Rigby*, as well as playing lots of Jazz standards. The next example is reminiscent of his style, played with a semi-swing feel. You are effectively playing two parts on one instrument, so be sure to practice the part of each hand separately before bringing it all together. The fretting hand plays the bass accompaniment, while the picking hand plays a melody or solo. It helps to play the tapped notes in a staccato manner, so you have more time to move around on the fretboard.

Example 5n

The next genre we're looking at is Country and there is a lot going on in this example. Bars 1-2 have a pedal steel line similar to examples 5b and 5c. In bar 3 there is a fluid sounding Albert Lee-style lick, and bar 4 shows an interesting approach to a popular cascading open string lick. By using both hands on the fretboard, you can get this sound in every key now. Watch the included video where I show you how to play this example fast and slow.

Example 5o

A mistake we often make as guitar players is to overplay, but in the real world it's more about choosing your moment. The following Soul groove is meant to be played without any bells and whistles, but once the song is over, you can end it with a beautiful lush sounding tapping lick.

Example 5p

Neo-Soul is a genre that has gained enormous popularity over the years and if you want to dig deeper into this style, check out *The Neo Soul Guitar Book* also published by **www.fundamental-changes.com**. The next example illustrates a fantastic way to include tapping tastefully in a Neo-Soul song or groove. There's also a new trick in this example, which is called "glitch tapping", invented by a true innovator of the tapping technique, Josh "Little Tybee" Martin.

The idea is to tap the same fret on the same string with multiple fingers, which creates a "glitchy" effect. In the first bar of the example below, this is notated as a tremolo picking effect and I suggest you start by executing this with two fingers of the picking hand, then build your way up to hitting the same note with three fingers. There's a lot going on in this example, so make sure you listen to the audio and watch the video.

Example 5q

In Pop, the most important thing is to just play the song, but there are often sections where a tapping lick can fit the style and add something special. The chord progression in Example 5r is fairly common, and I've added some tasteful tapping ideas to each of the three repetitions. Practice the tapping licks separately and focus on timing.

Example 5r

Another genre where tapping can be used to your advantage is Classical music and, by extension, Neo-Classical music, where tapping is used quite frequently already. Here is an example inspired by two popular Classical pieces: *Flight of the Bumblebee* by Rimsky-Korsakov and *Capriccio No. 5* by Paganini. If you like this kind of stuff, I encourage you to check out Paul Bielatowicz. He is an extremely accomplished arranger of Classical pieces for electric guitar. Of course, if you want this example to sound more Neo-Classical, just kick on the distortion and off you go. It may remind you of *Eugene's Trick Bag* from the movie *Crossroads*.

Example 5s

Here is an original Rock groove with flashy tapping licks that's meant to be played as tightly as possible.

Example 5t

And lastly, you can always combine ideas from different genres to create your own style. In this example, the goal is to let as many notes ring out as possible. Have fun with this lush sounding music and if necessary, watch the video and break this piece up into smaller fragments.

Example 5u

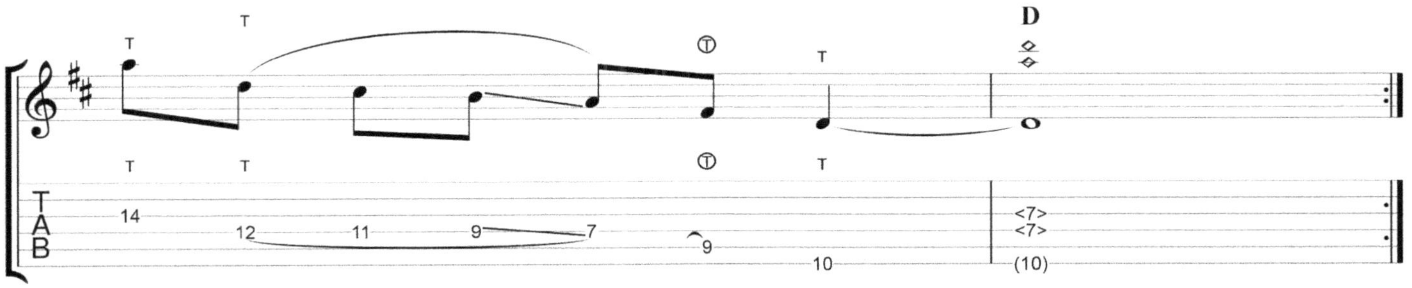
D
T
T
Ⓣ
T
T
T
Ⓣ
T
T
A
B
14
12
11
9
7
9
10
<7>
<7>
(10)

Conclusion

I hope you've enjoyed your tapping journey and have been inspired to add this technique to your bank of creative ideas. Tapping has a wide application, transcending musical style, and the tasteful application of this technique can set you apart as a player. I hope through this book, that you've also been able to expand your fretboard knowledge and visualization of the guitar neck, and that it has opened up new ideas to you.

As you continue to work on the material you've encountered, remember the all-important maxims of tapping:

- Accuracy

- Dampening

- Note separation and volume

- Timing

- Finger independence

Keep to a structured approach with your practice regime and you will reap the benefits for years to come.

Have fun!

Kristof

Other Books by Kristof Neyens

The Neo-Soul Guitar Book

The complete guide to the art of Neo-Soul guitar style and technique, featuring **Mark Lettieri.**

The Neo-Soul Guitar Book is a one-stop shop for the multi-faceted style of Neo-Soul guitar playing. In recent times Neo-Soul has emerged as a driving force in modern music, with notable players such as Mark Lettieri (three-time Grammy award winner) and Tom Misch reinventing Neo-Soul guitar for new audiences.

Neo-Soul is a mash up of RnB, Soul, Gospel and Funk, and is a wide ranging discipline. But authors Simon Pratt and Kristof Neyens have you covered – addressing every technique you need to become a top class Neo-Soul guitar player. In fact, whatever you play, this book is full of rut-busting ideas that can be applied to any style.

On top of that, this book features original pieces by Mark Lettieri of legendary band Snarky Puppy, as well as several other complete performance pieces – all of which are demonstrated with FREE accompanying video and audio to download.

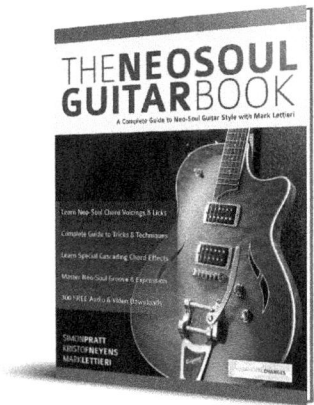

Guitar Looping: The Creative Guide

Artists like Ed Sheeran, Ellie Goulding and KT Tunstall use loopers as a key part of their live shows, and in this book Instagram guitar sensation Kristof Neyens shows you how to master looping with a wealth of creative ideas and cool licks and riffs. Though some musicians make it look easy, creating great loops is more challenging than it appears… but we've got you covered.

You'll discover how to build loops from the ground up; tricks to start and end loops perfectly every time; create killer, multiple-layer loops the right way, ensuring all parts fit together, and how to harmonise guitar parts.

But there's more...

- Use your looper to bust out of creative ruts
- How to lay down percussive grooves using your guitar as a drum
- Expressive techniques that will set you apart as a musician
- Simple but effective drop tuning techniques
- How to create synth-like pad effects to solo over
- How to mimic other instruments like violin, mandolin, pedal steel guitar, banjo and even clarinet
- How to use a slide to create unique loop parts
- Ways to imitate vinyl scratching, reverse loops and create other sound effects
- How to embrace randomness in loops and use it to your advantage
- Unique ways to combine other effects with your looper to create amazing soundscapes